DEMCO

# Soaps, Shampoos & Other Suds

....................................................................

*Make Beautiful Gifts to Give (or Keep)*

**KELLY RENO**

**PRIMA HOME**
**An Imprint of Prima Publishing**
3000 Lava Ridge Court
Roseville, California 95661
(800) 632-8676 • www.primalifestyles.com

PRIMA PUBLISHING® and its colophon are registered trademarks of Prima Communications, Inc. GOOD GIFTS FROM THE HOME is a trademark of Prima Communications, Inc.

DISCLAIMER: THE EXPRESS PURPOSE OF *SOAPS, SHAMPOOS & OTHER SUDS* IS TO PROVIDE SUGGESTIONS FOR A RECREATIONAL HOBBY. THE AUTHOR AND PUBLISHER DISCLAIM ANY WARRANTY OR GUARANTEE, EXPRESS OR IMPLIED, FOR ANY OF THE RECIPES OR FORMULAS CONTAINED HEREIN AND FURTHER DISCLAIM ANY LIABILITY FOR THE READER'S EXPERIMENTS OR PROJECTS. THE AUTHOR OR PUBLISHER DO NOT ASSUME ANY LIABILITY FOR ANY DAMAGES THAT MAY OCCUR AS A RESULT OF READING OR FOLLOWING ANY OF THE RECIPES OR FORMULAS IN THIS BOOK. THE PURCHASE OF THIS BOOK BY THE READER WILL SERVE AS AN ACKNOWLEDGMENT OF THIS DISCLAIMER AND AN AGREEMENT TO HOLD THE AUTHOR AND PUBLISHER HARMLESS FOR ANY MISTAKES THE READER MAY MAKE AS A RESULT OF FOLLOWING THE RECIPES AND FORMULAS IN THIS BOOK.

**Library of Congress Cataloging-in-Publication Data**

Reno, Kelly.
  Soaps, shampoos & other suds / by Kelly Reno.
    p.    cm. — (Good gifts from the home)

  Includes index.
  ISBN 0-7615-2543-2
  1. Soap.  2. Shampoo.  I. Title.  II. Series.
TP991.R38 1996                 95-44917
668'. 124—dc20                CIP

00  01  02  03  04  HH  10  9  8  7  6  5  4  3  2  1

Printed in the United States of America

**How to Order**

Single copies may be ordered from Prima Publishing, 3000 Lava Ridge Court, Roseville, CA 95661; telephone (800) 632-8676 ext. 4444. Quantity discounts are also available. On your letterhead, include information concerning the intended use of the books and the number of books you wish to purchase.

**Visit us online at www.primalifestyles.com**

. . . . . . . . . . . . . . . . . . . . . . . . . . . . . . . . . . . . . . . . . . . . . . . . . . . . . . . . . . . . . . . . . . . . . . . . . . . . . . . . . . . . . . . . . . . .

❦ Dedicated to the O'Rourke Family

# CONTENTS

**ACKNOWLEDGMENTS**  vii

**INTRODUCTION**  viii

**CHAPTER 1**  *Soaps*  1

**CHAPTER 2**  *Shampoos*  31

**CHAPTER 3**  *For the Bath*  43

**CHAPTER 4**  *Hair Conditioners*  57

**CHAPTER 5**  *Products for Children*  63

**CHAPTER 6**  *Gift Wrapping*  73

*Marketplace*  79

*Index*  83

# ACKNOWLEDGMENTS

............................................................................................

I THANK my husband, Fred, for his support and for acting as my number one research subject. Many times he gladly accepted bottles of my concoctions while walking to the shower and he always provided me with an honest opinion. His help in my research has been invaluable. Fred also took over the operation of our two businesses, which freed up my time so that I could complete this project.

I also want to thank my friends and family, who have given me encouragement by their delighted reactions after trying my recipes.

............................................................................................

❧ WHAT STARTED out as a hobby has developed into a complete book of recipes for shampoos, soaps, and other bubbling luxuries. I found myself confused after trying to make sense of the chemical gibberish on the labels of shampoo bottles. I wanted to know exactly what all of those ingredients with the long names were and how I could make them myself. I began an extensive researching campaign by reading many technical books on formulas and remedies. Eventually I discovered what cosmetics are really made out of. Through trial and error, I was able to replace the chemical and synthetic components with natural and accessible ingredients so that the average person could duplicate commercially prepared formulas in his or her very own kitchen.

Besides being economical and easy to make, my recipes make wonderful gifts, which you, too, will discover after giving friends and family bottles of sudsy, fragrant concoctions that you've created. This book is not about aromatherapy or herbal remedies. Rather, it is a useful cookbook designed for the ordinary person. You'll find that my recipes make products comparable to the commercially prepared formulas and most have a shelf life of over a year without preservatives.

Making cosmetics at home not only is great fun, but you'll feel good about the things that you make because you know exactly what ingredients were used

............................................................................................

and precisely what you're putting on your body. The mystery of a long, confusing list of chemical ingredients is over and the secrets to fabulous soaps and suds are revealed!

In this book, I give you original recipes for bubbling luxuries. You'll also find useful information for creative ideas about gift wrapping and bottling your creations. A marketplace section has been included in the book so that everyone has access to some of the harder-to-find ingredients by mail order.

Your friends will be delighted to receive a homemade package of sweet-smelling soaps, shampoos, shower gels, hair conditioners, and many other unique products. All of the suggested fragrances and colors in the recipes can be altered by replacing one fragrance oil with another. For example, you can make a whole line of rose-fragranced products such as soap, shampoo, and conditioner simply by replacing the suggested fragrance oil with an equal amount of rose fragrance oil. This will allow you the freedom to create very personalized gifts suited to the fragrance tastes of your gift recipients. Thoughts of you will linger every time your friends use your luxurious products and you'll probably get requests for second and third batches! They might not even believe that you made them yourself!

..............................................................................................

If you can bear to part with your spectacular creations, you'll find that these formulas make excellent and economical presents for birthdays, holidays, thank-yous, and any other occasion. Remember to keep a few bottles around for yourself as a pampering treat. The research is done and the recipes are here in this book for you to use. Enjoy!

..............................................................................................

# CHAPTER ONE

# Soaps

THE SOAP recipes you'll find in this book have been specially designed to create wonderful gourmet and specialty soaps with very little trouble. Traditionally, soaps are made from water and oil and are melded together with lye and can take several weeks to age. The recipes in this book are created from two types of pure soap bases and can be made and ready to use in just a few hours.

## Castile Soap

*Castile soap* is the oldest and purest soap in existence and can be found in health food stores. Named after the Castile region of Spain, where it originated hundreds of years ago, it is made from water and olive oil and has a white to green color. It comes in cake bars and has virtually no scent, making it an ideal base soap. Castile soap needs to be shredded before melting it with other ingredients. Use a cheese grater for easy shredding.

❧ *Castile soap can be replaced with baby soap or any other plain, unscented white soap in these recipes.*

## Glycerin Soap

*Glycerin soap* is made from oil and glycerin and can be purchased in an unscented form from most grocery or health food stores. Be sure to buy the unscented bars. Glycerin soap is usually yellowish and transparent. It makes an ideal base for gourmet soaps, as it melts easily and mixes well with oils and other ingredients. You will also find glycerin soap very easy to shape.

❧ *When melting glycerin soap do not heat to over 160°F or your finished soap will "sweat."*

........................................................................

## Molding Soaps

Once you've mixed your soap, you'll need a mold to pour or pack it into while the soap is still warm. You can buy molds made especially for soap or you can make your own. An empty tuna can makes a great mold for a round soap. You can also use an empty milk carton to make a square-shaped soap. Candy molds and muffin tins make wonderful decorative soap molds.

Pour or pack the soap into its mold and let it harden. The next step is to separate the soap from its container. If you've used a milk carton, you could just peel the carton away. If the soap is in a tuna can, either open the bottom of the can and push the soap out, or try popping it out (like popping ice cubes out of a tray).

For harder, longer-lasting soaps, remove the soaps from their molds and set them out to air dry for a couple of days.

## How to Protect Your Soaps and Make Them Last

Homemade soaps make wonderful gifts. Choosing a personalized blend for friends is an easy and inexpensive way to create special presents that will be remembered every time they suds up with your heavenly soap.

........................................................................

To protect your special soaps, wrap them with clear cellophane twenty-four hours (six hours minimum) after you remove them from their molds. For more gift-wrapping ideas, see the chapter near the end of this book.

## *Making the Soap Last Longer*

Soap tends to melt away when left in a puddle of water. The following instructions for making soap on a rope will extend its life. Soap can be hung on a cord or decorative satin ribbon from your shower head or water spout. Adding cord or ribbon to your soap is ultimately economical and a nice touch when giving soaps as gifts. All you'll need to make soap on a rope is a twenty-inch piece of nylon cord or satin ribbon and a plastic drinking straw.

## *Ingredients*

Borax can be found in the laundry section in grocery stores. Beeswax is available from suppliers listed in the marketplace section in the back of the book, and liquid lanolin can be found in health food stores that carry beauty supplies. Fragrance oils, herbs, and clays can be found in health food stores or ordered from suppliers listed in the marketplace section in the back of the book.

❧ *For glycerin-based soap*   When the soap has set, push a drinking straw through the center of the soap, then pull it out gently. You should now have a clean hole through it.

❧ *For Castile-based soap*   Pour your soap into the mold. While the soap is still soft, push a drinking straw through the center until it touches the bottom of the mold. Leave the straw in the soap until it has set. Remove the straw just before you take the soap out of the mold.

*Now that you have a hole in your soap, do the following:*

1.  Run one end of the cord or ribbon through the hole.
2.  Bring the two ends together and tie in a knot around the soap.
3.  Bring the two ends together again and tie into another knot so that you have a large loop from which to hang your soap.

## OATMEAL SOAP

......................................................................

❦ *This soap is a favorite for facial and body cleansing. Made with pure Castile soap, skin-nourishing oatmeal, and essential oils, this fabulous soap is "breakfast for your skin." I'm almost always asked to make a second batch for delighted friends who have tried my Oatmeal Soap.*

Makes one bar

    4-ounce bar Castile soap, shredded
    ¼ cup dried oats
    ¼ cup distilled water
    1 tablespoon dried chamomile
    1 tablespoon dried rosemary
    1 tablespoon jojoba oil

Shred the Castile soap and set aside. Grind the oats into a fine powder in a food processor or coffee grinder and set aside. In a saucepan, bring the water to a boil. Remove the pan from the heat and place the chamomile and rosemary in a tea strainer in the water, letting it steep for thirty minutes to create a strong herbal infusion. Remove the herbs from the water and reheat to a boil. Turn the heat down to low and add the shredded Castile soap a little at a time while stirring. Continue stirring until the mixture forms a sticky mass. Remove the pan from heat and stir in the oat powder and jojoba oil until evenly distributed. Pack the soap into a mold and let it set for four hours or until hardened.

## HERBAL FANTASY SOAP

........................................................................

❦ *This recipe makes one bar of the most wonderful soap on earth. Infused with herbal goodness and flowers, it does wonders for the complexion. This soap works as an exfoliant and gives your skin the benefits of natural plant extracts and nourishing oils.*

Makes one bar

   4-ounce bar Castile soap
   2 teaspoons dried rose petals
   1 teaspoon dried chamomile
   1 teaspoon dried peppermint leaves
   1 teaspoon dried orange blossoms
   1 teaspoon dried lemongrass
   1 tablespoon sesame oil
   1 coffee filter
   ¼ cup distilled water

........................................................................

Shred the Castile soap and set aside. Place the dried herbs and flowers in a coffee filter, securing it with a piece of string. In a heavy saucepan, heat the water to a boil. Remove the pan from the heat and add the herbs. Let steep for one hour. Remove herbs from water and return the pan to the stove and boil. Stir the shredded soap into the water and herbs. Add the sesame oil to the mixture and stir until it forms a sticky mass. Pack the soap into its mold and let set for five hours or until hardened.

# PEPPERMINT AND CHAMOMILE SOAP

........................................................................

❦ *This fun and fragrant soap is enjoyed by adults as well as children. The gentle blend is especially good for tired, aching muscles and its fresh peppermint aroma calms and relaxes after a long day.*

Makes one bar

> 4-ounce bar Castile soap
> ¼ cup distilled water
> 2 tablespoons dried chamomile
> 1 drop red food coloring (optional)
> 1 tablespoon liquid lanolin
> 1 teaspoon jojoba oil
> 10 drops peppermint oil
> 4 drops vitamin E oil (can squeeze out of capsule)

........................................................................

Shred the Castile soap and set aside. Bring the water to a boil in a heavy saucepan and add the chamomile. Remove the pan from the heat and let the chamomile steep for twenty minutes. Pour the water through a strainer, collecting the water in a bowl (this removes the chamomile). Pour the water back into the saucepan and reheat the water, bringing it to a boil. Add the food coloring (if desired) to the water and stir until evenly distributed. Lower the heat and add the soap chips. Stir until it forms a sticky mass. Add the lanolin, jojoba oil, peppermint oil, and vitamin E oil and stir until well mixed. Remove the soap from the heat and pack into a mold. Let set for six hours or until the soap hardens.

...........................................................................................

❦ *This soap is a favorite for cleaning up dirty, dry hands after a day of gardening. Made with rosemary and lavender, Gardener's Friend Hand Soap soothes tired hands while the cornmeal acts as a gentle scrubbing agent that removes dirt from the skin. Although it isn't one of the prettier soaps (it looks grainy and is greenish-brown in color), it does an excellent job and makes your hands feel wonderful.*

❦ *Gardener's Friend Hand Soap makes a great, personalized gift for green-thumbed friends.*

Makes one bar

   4-ounce bar Castile soap
   ⅔ cup distilled water
   2 tablespoons dried lavender
   2 tablespoons dried rosemary
   3 tablespoons yellow cornmeal
   1 teaspoon liquid lanolin
   5 drops lavender oil

Shred the soap and set aside. Boil the water in a heavy saucepan over low heat and add the dried lavender and rosemary. Remove the pan from the heat and let the herbs steep for thirty minutes. Strain out the herbs and reheat the water, bringing it to a boil. Stir in the shredded soap and lower the heat. Continue stirring until the mixture forms a sticky mass. Remove the pan from the heat and add the cornmeal, lanolin, and lavender oil, stirring until well mixed. Spoon the mixture into a soap mold and let set for six hours or until hardened.

❧ *Try using Peach and Berry Gardener's Hand Cream (the next recipe) after washing your hands with this soap for super soft hands.*

...............................................................................................

❦ *This fragrant, heavy-duty hand cream is a favorite of gardeners because of its thick, coating texture. It also doubles as a body moisturizer to protect problem dry areas such as elbows and knees. As a gift, you can replace the fragrance oils with equal amounts of your gardening friend's favorite floral fragrance oil, such as rose or lavender.*

Makes 8 ounces

½ cup distilled water
⅛ teaspoon borax powder
⅓ cup sweet almond oil
1 tablespoon liquid lanolin
1 teaspoon coconut oil
1 tablespoon beeswax, grated
10 drops raspberry fragrance oil
10 drops peach fragrance oil

Combine the water and borax in a heavy saucepan and heat until the borax has dissolved completely. Let it simmer gently while preparing the next step. In a separate saucepan, combine the almond oil, lanolin, coconut oil, and beeswax and heat until the wax has melted and the ingredients are well blended. Pour the oil mixture into a ceramic bowl and slowly add the heated water and borax mixture, stirring with a wire whisk. Continue stirring the mixture until it becomes a thick, white cream and has cooled to room temperature. Stir in the fragrance oils and pour into a bottle or jar. Seal tightly.

🌸 *When making creams, it is imperative to add the water/borax mixture to the oil/wax mixture very slowly—about a teaspoonful at a time—to prevent separation.*

## MUD SOAP

........................................................................

❧ *This soap is great for cleansing away grime and dirt from the skin. The formula is gentle, yet cleans deeply and tightens the pores without drying.*

    ❧ *Mud soap makes a good body soap for men.*

Makes one bar

    4-ounce bar Castile soap
    ¼ cup distilled water
    1 teaspoon liquid glycerin
    5 drops sandalwood oil (optional)
    1 tablespoon fuller's earth
        (can substitute with powdered French clay)

Shred the Castile soap and set it aside. Bring the water to a boil in a heavy saucepan, then reduce heat and simmer. Stir in the glycerin and sandalwood oil (if desired) and remove the pan from the heat. Add fuller's earth, stirring until dissolved. Stir in the shredded soap chips and continue mixing until it forms a sticky mass. Pack the soap into its mold and let set for six hours or until hardened.

........................................................................

. . . . . . . . . . . . . . . . . . . . . . . . . . . . . . . . . . . . . . . . . . . . . . . . . . . . . . . . . . . . . . . . . . . . . . . . . . .

*This soap is a nice formula to use in the bath or shower. Rice bran has been used in the Orient for thousands of years to cleanse and soften the skin and has contributed to milky, clear complexions. The coarse texture of the rice bran added to this unique bath soap makes a wonderful treat that's gentle enough for everyday use.*

Makes one bar

> 4-ounce bar Castile soap
> ⅓ cup soy milk
> 4 tablespoons rice bran
> 5 drops jasmine fragrance oil

Shred the soap and set aside. In a heavy saucepan over low heat, warm the soy milk and gradually add the shredded soap until the mixture becomes a sticky mass. Remove the pan from the heat and add the rice bran and jasmine oil, stirring until the bran is evenly distributed. Spoon the soap into a mold and let set for four hours or until hardened.

*For an extra large body bar, double the above recipe and use an empty milk carton as a soap mold.*

. . . . . . . . . . . . . . . . . . . . . . . . . . . . . . . . . . . . . . . . . . . . . . . . . . . . . . . . . . . . . . . . . . . . . . . . . . .

.........................................................................

❦ *This soap captures the pure essence of Georgia's prized peaches. A fragrant, milky treat, perfect for all-over body cleansing.*

Makes one bar

> 4-ounce bar Castile soap
> ¼ cup distilled water
> ¼ cup powdered milk
> 1 tablespoon sweet almond oil
> ⅛ teaspoon peach fragrance oil
> 1 drop orange food coloring (optional)

Shred the Castile soap and set aside. Heat the water in a heavy saucepan over low heat. Stir in the shredded soap until it forms a sticky mass. Remove the pan from the heat and add the powdered milk, sweet almond oil, peach fragrance oil, and food coloring until well blended. Spoon the soap into its mold and let set for four hours or until hardened.

.........................................................................

# VANILLA AND ALMOND SOAP

............................................................

❦ *This soap makes a fragrant bar of super scrubbing soap. It is specially designed to remove dirt and oil from the skin without drying. Vanilla gives it a delicious fragrance and the ground almonds provide a beautifully textured soap.*

Makes one bar

> ⅓ cup whole almonds
> 4-ounce bar Castile soap
> ¼ cup distilled water
> 1 tablespoon almond oil
> ⅛ teaspoon vanilla fragrance oil

Grind the almonds to a fine powder in a food processor or coffee grinder and set aside. Shred the soap and set aside. In a heavy saucepan bring the water to a boil, then reduce heat to a simmer. Add the shredded soap to the water and stir until it forms a sticky mass. Remove the pan from the heat and add the almond powder, almond oil, and vanilla fragrance oil, stirring until well blended. Spoon the soap into a mold and let set for five hours or until hardened.

............................................................

## CREAMSICLE SOAP

........................................................................

❦ *Remember indulging in a creamy orange and vanilla Creamsicle bar on a hot summer day? Now you can enjoy it all over again, without the calories! This soap was inspired by the popular frozen treat and is perfect for anyone young at heart. This recipe creates two luxurious bars of Creamsicle Soap, so there will be one for you and one for a friend. Lightly scented with a fun orange and vanilla fragrance and made with real cream, this soap is gentle enough for all skin types.*

❦ *You'll need two soap molds*

Makes two bars

> Two 4-ounce bars unscented glycerin soap
> 10 drops orange oil
> 1 drop orange food coloring
> 3 tablespoons heavy whipping cream
> 10 drops vanilla fragrance oil

In a heavy saucepan over low heat, melt one bar of glycerin soap until liquefied. Remove the pan from the heat and add the orange oil and food coloring, stirring until well mixed. Pour half of the mixture into each soap mold and let it set for one hour. When the orange soap has set, melt the second bar of glycerin soap until liquefied. Remove the pan from the heat and stir in the whipping cream and vanilla fragrance oil. Pour the melted soap into the molds on top of the orange soap. Let it set for three hours. Your finished bars should come out half orange and half white.

# LEMON LOOFAH SOAP

........................................................

🍋 *Lemon Loofah Soap was designed to exfoliate dry skin from the body. Its fresh, clean citrus fragrance gives the skin a natural lift while the glycerin base soothes. The scrubbing action of the natural loofah sponge has been used for hundreds of years. Loofahs are dried plants closely related to cucumber, and are used to scrub away dry and dead skin cells.*

Makes one bar

> Dried loofah sponge
>    (1 square inch)
> 4-ounce bar unscented glycerin soap
> 1 teaspoon liquid lanolin
> 1 teaspoon aloe vera gel
> 15 drops lemon oil
> 1 drop yellow food coloring

With a pair of sharp scissors, cut off one square inch of loofah sponge. Shred the loofah sponge into tiny pieces, either in a coffee grinder or with scissors, and set aside. In a heavy saucepan over low heat, melt the bar of glycerin soap, stirring constantly until liquefied. Remove the pan from the heat and add the lanolin, aloe vera gel, lemon oil, and food coloring, stirring until well mixed. Immediately add the shredded loofah and stir until evenly distributed. Pour into a mold and let set for three hours or until hardened.

## COFFEE AND CREAM SOAP

*Coffee acts as one of nature's sunscreens. This soap is great to use before going out in the sun, and also makes a great morning wake-up soap for coffee lovers. The soap captures the essence of freshly ground coffee and will smell of it while being used, but won't leave behind a scent or stain the skin. It has a beautiful, deep brown coloring.*

*If you plan to be in the sun for long, you should use a sunscreen to prevent burning.*

Makes one bar

> 2 teaspoons coffee beans
>   (can replace with 1 teaspoon instant espresso)
> 4-ounce bar unscented glycerin soap
> 1 teaspoon heavy whipping cream
> 1 teaspoon aloe vera gel

Grind two teaspoons of your favorite coffee beans to espresso grade in a coffee grinder. Melt the glycerin soap over low heat in a heavy saucepan until liquefied. Remove the pan from the heat and add the ground coffee, whipping cream, and aloe vera, stirring until well blended. Pour the mixture into a mold and let set for three hours or until hardened.

# CINNAMON SOAP

............................................................

❧ *"Sugar and spice and everything nice" comes to mind when sudsing up with this delightfully fragrant soap. Its ruby red color and heavenly scent make bath time an event to look forward to.*

❧ *This recipe is perfect for making miniature soaps in decorative candy molds.*

Makes one bar

4-ounce bar unscented glycerin soap
10 drops cinnamon oil
1 drop red food coloring (optional)

In a heavy saucepan, melt the glycerin soap over low heat until liquefied. Remove the pan from the heat and stir in the cinnamon oil and coloring until well mixed. Pour the soap into a mold and let set for three hours.

............................................................

. . . . . . . . . . . . . . . . . . . . . . . . . . . . . . . . . . . . . . . . . . . . . . . . . . . . . . . . . . . . . .

❦ *Raspberry Oat Powder Soap makes a great face and body cleanser. The nondrying glycerin base is soothing to the skin while the oat powder gently removes impurities.*

Makes one bar

> ⅓ cup dried oats
> 4-ounce bar unscented glycerin soap
> 15 drops raspberry fragrance oil
> 1 drop red food coloring (optional)

Grind the oats to a fine powder in a food processor and set aside. In a heavy saucepan over low heat, melt the glycerin soap until liquefied. Remove the pan from the heat and add the raspberry fragrance oil, red food coloring (if desired), and oat powder, stirring until well mixed. Pour into a soap mold and let set for three hours or until hardened.

. . . . . . . . . . . . . . . . . . . . . . . . . . . . . . . . . . . . . . . . . . . . . . . . . . . . . . . . . . . . . .

# TOMATO AND BAKING SODA SOAP

. . . . . . . . . . . . . . . . . . . . . . . . . . . . . . . . . . . . . . . . . . . . . . . . . . . . . . . . . . . . . . . . . . . . . . . . . . . . . . . . . . . . . . . . .

❦ *Tomato and Baking Soda Soap was designed to cleanse and tighten the skin's pores. Made with oil-absorbing tomato juice and cleansing baking powder, this soap works wonders on normal to oily skin.*

Makes one bar

      4-ounce bar unscented glycerin soap
      5 tablespoons tomato juice
      ½ teaspoon red wine vinegar
      15 drops lemon oil
      1 teaspoon baking soda

In a heavy saucepan over low heat, melt the glycerin soap until liquefied. Stir in the tomato juice, red wine vinegar, and lemon oil. Remove the pan from the heat. Stir in the baking soda until dissolved. Pour the soap into a mold and let set for three hours or until hardened.

## ROSE COLD CREAM SOAP

.........................................................................

❧ *Rose Cold Cream Soap is a gentle cleansing bar infused with moisturizing cold cream to soothe the skin. It leaves the skin lightly fragranced and as soft as rose petals.*

Makes one bar

> 4-ounce bar unscented glycerin soap
> 2 teaspoons cold cream
> (see the following recipe)
> 10 drops rose fragrance oil
> 1 drop red food coloring (optional)

In a heavy saucepan over low heat, melt the glycerin soap until liquefied. Stir in the cold cream until dissolved, then remove the pan from the heat. Stir in the rose fragrance oil and food coloring (if desired). Pour into a mold and let set for four hours or until hardened.

## COLD CREAM

........................................................................................................

❦ *This thick, moisture-rich cold cream is a pampering remedy for dry skin. The recipe is an updated version of a very old beeswax beauty cream used by the ancient Greeks.*

Makes 8 ounces

> ¼ cup distilled water
> ⅛ teaspoon borax powder
> 3 tablespoons beeswax, grated
> ½ cup mineral oil
> 1 teaspoon coconut oil

In a heavy saucepan, bring the water to a boil and add the borax, stirring until dissolved. Simmer gently while performing the next step. In another heavy saucepan melt the beeswax, mineral oil, and coconut oil over low heat, until a clear liquid forms. Pour the hot oil and beeswax mixture into a ceramic bowl. Slowly pour in the heated water and borax mixture, stirring constantly with a wire whisk. Continue stirring until the mixture forms a very thick white cream. Continue stirring until it cools to room temperature. Spoon into a jar and seal.

........................................................................................................

# CHAPTER TWO

# *Shampoos*

SHAMPOOING IS the first step to beautiful and healthy hair. Shampoos by definition are preparations for cleaning the hair and scalp of impurities. An effective shampoo will cleanse the hair of dirt, oil, and build-up that can make it appear dull and lifeless. In this chapter you will find recipes for wonderful shampoos and shower gels that have a long shelf life and make fabulous, personalized gifts. To make great products like the ones on the market, you can purchase special shampoo concentrates (see the marketplace section near the end of this book) or you can use a ready-made, unscented shampoos available in most health food stores.

By making your own shampoos and shower gels, you could save hundreds of dollars a year and will have the freedom to create special, all-natural formulas that are good for the hair and skin. The special ingredients that you will need are called *foaming agents*; they form the sudsy basis of all shampoo products. Foaming agents lather well and allow water to spread out and penetrate the hair and skin. They are derived from natural ingredients, such as coconut oil and alcohols, through a special process. All regular and organic shampoos and shower gels on the market today contain foaming agents that are completely safe and nontoxic.

In the recipes that follow, you will find that table salt is called for. Salt increases the viscosity (or thickness) of liquid soap. Fragrance oils and herbs called for in these recipes can be purchased from most health food stores or ordered from the suppliers listed in the marketplace section in the back of the book.

# LIQUID SHAMPOO AND SHOWER GEL BASE

........................................................................

❦ *Liquid Shampoo and Shower Gel Base, and Gel Shampoo Base (see the following page) provide the basis for the recipes that follow. See mixing instructions in each recipe.*

Makes 8 ounces

¾ cup distilled water
¼ cup shampoo concentrate
(or substitute with ½ cup unscented shampoo and
increase salt to 1 teaspoon)
½ teaspoon table salt

........................................................................

## GEL SHAMPOO BASE

........................................................................

Makes 8 ounces

¾ cup distilled water
¼ cup shampoo concentrate
(or substitute ½ cup unscented shampoo and
increase salt to 1½ teaspoons)
1 teaspoon table salt

## LEMON SPARKLE SHAMPOO

........................................................................................

❦ *Lemon Sparkle Shampoo has been specially designed for daily use on all hair types. The gentle formula contains soothing herbs and scalp-stimulating lemon oil that leave the hair shiny and clean.*

Makes 8½ ounces

> Ingredients for Liquid Shampoo and Shower Gel Base
> (recipe on page 33)
> 2 tablespoons dried chamomile
> 1 tablespoon dried rosemary
> 2 teaspoons sweet almond oil
> ¼ teaspoon lemon oil
> 1 drop yellow food coloring (optional)

Heat the water in a saucepan, bringing it to a boil. Add dried chamomile and rosemary to the water and remove the pan from the heat. Let the herbs sit in the water for twenty minutes. Pour the water through a strainer and into a collecting bowl. Discard the herbs. Add the shampoo concentrate to the water and stir until it has dissolved. Add the almond oil, lemon oil, and food coloring (if desired) and stir until blended. Add the salt and stir until the mixture thickens. Let the mixture cool to room temperature and bottle.

........................................................................................

.......................................................................

❧ *Specially designed to correct split ends, this formula is rich with silky hair-strengthening oils to help restore luster, shine, and elasticity, making your hair more manageable and less brittle. Coconut and Vanilla Hair Repair Shampoo is a good choice for daily use.*

Makes 9 ounces

> Ingredients for Gel Shampoo Base
>   (recipe on page 34)
> 1 tablespoon coconut oil
> 2 teaspoons jojoba oil
> 10 drops vanilla fragrance oil
> 10 drops coconut fragrance oil

Warm the water and add the shampoo concentrate, stirring until well blended. Add the coconut oil, jojoba oil, salt, vanilla fragrance oil, and coconut fragrance oil and stir with a wire whisk until the mixture becomes a smooth, thick liquid. Pour into a bottle and seal.

> ❧ *A plastic squeeze bottle works best for this gel shampoo.*

.......................................................................

# PEPPERMINT CLARIFYING SHAMPOO

......................................................................

❦ *Peppermint Clarifying Shampoo is a tingly treat for all hair types. Made with fragrant peppermint essential oil and nutrient-rich jojoba oil, it stimulates the scalp without drying and helps to remove build-up.*

❦ *This shampoo is great for revitalizing the hair after a work-out and will help restore its bounciness and manageability.*

Makes 8½ ounces

Ingredients for Liquid Shampoo and Shower Gel Base
(see recipe on page 33)
2 teaspoons jojoba oil
⅛ teaspoon peppermint oil
1 drop red food coloring (optional)

Warm the water and pour into a ceramic bowl. Add the shampoo concentrate and stir with a wire whisk until well blended. Add the salt, jojoba oil, peppermint oil, and food coloring (if desired) and stir until well blended. Pour into a bottle and close.

......................................................................

.........................................................................

❦ *This shampoo is an effective solution for removing impurities such as smog and city grime from the hair. The nondrying formula includes a selection of special plant extracts and oils that were chosen to deep-clean and protect your hair. Ylang Ylang and cinnamon oils create a unique and invigorating fragrance.*

Makes 8½ ounces

Ingredients for Liquid Shampoo and Shower Gel Base
   (recipe on page 33)
1 tablespoon dried thyme
1 tablespoon dried peppermint
1 teaspoon dried lavender
1 teaspoon witch hazel
1 teaspoon almond oil
7 drops cinnamon oil
3 drops Ylang Ylang oil

.........................................................................

In a heavy saucepan, bring the water to a boil and add the dried thyme, peppermint, and lavender. Remove the pan from the heat and let steep for thirty minutes. Strain the herbs from the water and pour the herbally infused water into a ceramic bowl. Add the shampoo concentrate and stir until well mixed. Add the salt, witch hazel, almond oil, cinnamon oil, and Ylang Ylang oil to the mixture, stirring until thick. Bottle and close.

# EMERGENCY SHAMPOO

........................................................................

❦ *Running out of shampoo can be quite an inconvenience. If you don't feel like making an emergency trip to the store, stay home instead and make a quick batch of emergency shampoo from ingredients you probably have in your kitchen.*

Makes about 8 ounces

> ¾ cup water
> 3 tablespoons dishwashing liquid or liquid soap
> 1 teaspoon table salt
> 1 teaspoon mineral oil
>     (can substitute with any vegetable oil)
> 10 drops fragrance oil (optional)

Heat water in a saucepan and add liquid soap, stirring until well mixed. Add the salt and mineral oil, stirring until the mixture thickens. Add the fragrance oil (if desired) and stir. Bottle.

❦ *You can use unscented dish-washing liquid or liquid soap, which are available at some health food stores. Add ten drops of your favorite fragrance oil if desired.*

❦ *To make Emergency Lemon Shampoo, use lemon-scented dishwashing liquid and add ten drops of lemon oil.*

........................................................................

# OLD-FASHIONED SHAMPOO

...................................................................

❦ *In the olden days, people used to wash their hair with bars of pure Castile soap. In the early 1930s, liquid shampoos replaced the old Castile bars. This recipe is for an old-fashioned cream shampoo made with a Castile soap base. This original recipe makes an unscented shampoo, but you can add about ten drops of fragrance oil or perfume to it if you desire.*

Makes 9½ ounces

> 1 cup distilled water
> 3 tablespoons Castile soap, shredded
> 10 drops fragrance oil (optional)

Bring water to a boil in a heavy saucepan, then reduce the heat to a simmer. Add the shredded Castile soap and stir until the soap has dissolved. Add the fragrance oil (if desired). Let cool to room temperature and bottle.

   ❦ *Apply Old-Fashioned Lemon Rinse (the next recipe) after using this shampoo to remove soap build-up.*
   ❦ *Don't expect lots of bubbly suds from this shampoo.*

...................................................................

# OLD-FASHIONED LEMON RINSE

········································································

❦ *This recipe was specially designed to remove soap build-up from the hair. Pour the rinse over your hair after using Old-Fashioned Shampoo and gently massage it in. Rinse with warm water.*

Makes 5 ounces

    ½ cup water
    2 tablespoons lemon juice

Combine the ingredients in a bottle and shake until well mixed. This recipe makes enough for one rinse.

········································································

# CHAPTER THREE

# For the Bath

IN THIS CHAPTER you will find many recipes for deliciously fragrant bubble baths, bath oils, shower gels, and many other unique formulas that all make delightful gifts. I often make up gift baskets for friends and fill them with soaps, shower gels, and other bath-time luxuries. Bathing for many is a time to escape temporarily from the turbulent world outside. You can enhance bath time for friends and family by creating these personalized and treasured gifts, using my unique formulas. From fruity fresh scents to relaxing florals, you'll find a recipe for everyone.

. . . . . . . . . . . . . . . . . . . . . . . . . . . . . . . . . . . . . . . . . . . . . . . . .

❦ *In Green Apple and Aloe Vera Shower Gel the essence of fresh green apples has been captured in a nourishing base of aloe vera. This sudsy formula is ideal for total body cleansing and can also be used as a shampoo.*

Makes 9 ounces

> Ingredients for Liquid Shampoo and Shower Gel Base
>   (see recipe on page 33)
> 2 tablespoons aloe vera gel
> 15 drops apple fragrance oil
> 1 drop green food coloring (optional)

Warm the water and pour into a ceramic bowl. Add the shampoo concentrate and stir until well mixed. Add the aloe vera gel, salt, apple fragrance oil, and coloring (if desired) and stir until thick and well blended. Pour into a squeeze bottle and cap.

. . . . . . . . . . . . . . . . . . . . . . . . . . . . . . . . . . . . . . . . . . . . . . . . .

# GEORGIA PEACH SHOWER GEL

...................................................................................

✻ *This fun and fruity shower gel captures the essence of freshly picked peaches. You'll have Georgia on your mind when you lather up with this skin-nourishing formula enriched with vitamin E and essential apricot oil.*

Makes 8½ ounces

> Ingredients for Liquid Shampoo and Shower Gel Base
>    (see recipe on page 33)
> 1 tablespoon apricot kernel oil
> 15 drops peach fragrance oil
> 5 drops vitamin E oil (can use 2 capsules)
> 1 drop orange food coloring (optional)

Warm the water and pour into a ceramic bowl. Add the shampoo concentrate, stirring until well blended. Add the apricot kernel oil, salt, peach fragrance oil, vitamin E oil (just break open the capsules), and coloring (if desired), stirring until well blended and thick. Pour into a squeeze bottle and close.

...................................................................................

❧ *This nourishing formula cleanses gently, giving the skin the benefits of milk, an old-fashioned treatment for the complexion.*

Makes 9 ounces

> Ingredients for Liquid Shampoo and Shower Gel Base
>   (see recipe on page 33)
> 2 tablespoons powdered milk
> 10 drops lavender oil
> 1 drop violet food coloring (optional)

Warm the water and pour into a ceramic bowl. Stir in the powdered milk. Add the shampoo concentrate and salt, stirring until well blended and thick. Add the milk, lavender oil, and food coloring (if desired), stirring until well mixed. Pour into a squeeze bottle and cap.

# WILD GARDEN SHOWER SOAP

..................................................................................................

❦ *Wild Garden Shower Soap, made with natural herbs and flowers, gently cleanses the skin and has a fresh scent. It's ideal for everyday use.*

Makes 8½ ounces

> ½ cup distilled water
> ½ cup orange flower water
> 1 tablespoon dried peppermint leaves
> 1 tablespoon dried chamomile
> 1 tablespoon dried rose petals
> 1 tablespoon dried orange blossoms
> ½ tablespoon unscented glycerin soap
> 1 teaspoon castor oil

Combine the distilled water and orange flower water in a saucepan and bring to a boil. Remove the pan from the heat and add the dried peppermint, chamomile, rose petals, and orange blossoms. Let steep for one hour. Strain the herbs and flowers from the water and reheat gently. Add the glycerin soap and stir until dissolved. Remove the saucepan from the heat and stir in the castor oil. Let cool to room temperature and bottle.

..................................................................................................

# EASY SHOWER GEL

........................................................................

❦ *If you don't have the time to order special shampoo concentrates, you can make your own thick and rich shower gel using a regular, unscented shampoo.*

Makes 8 ounces

> ¾ cup distilled water
> ¼ cup unscented shampoo
> 1 teaspoon table salt
> 15 drops fragrance oil

In a saucepan, heat the water gently and stir in the shampoo until dissolved. Add the salt and stir until the mixture becomes thick and well blended. Add the fragrance oil and stir. Bottle.

........................................................................

# HONEY AND ROSE WATER FACE WASH

........................................................

❦ *This foaming face wash combines honey (a natural antibacterial agent) and rose water (nature's astringent) in a foaming face wash. Honey and Rose Water Face Wash gently removes make-up and impurities as it moisturizes the skin.*

Makes 9 ounces

⅔ cup distilled water
¼ cup shampoo concentrate
   (or substitute ½ cup unscented shampoo
   and increase the salt to 1 teaspoon)
2 tablespoons honey
2 tablespoons rose water
½ teaspoon table salt

Warm the water and add the shampoo concentrate, stirring until well mixed. Add the honey, rose water, and salt, stirring until thick and well blended. Bottle.

........................................................

# LEMON AND MINT FACE WASH

......................................................................

❦ *This cleansing face wash is ideal for everyday use. Lemon and peppermint add a refreshing fragrance and promote healthy skin. Made with pure glycerin soap and mineral water, this gentle formula is good for all skin types.*

Makes 9 ounces

    1 cup mineral water
    ½ tablespoon unscented glycerin soap
    5 drops lemon oil
    5 drops peppermint oil

In a heavy saucepan bring the water to a boil and add the glycerin soap, stirring until the soap has dissolved. Remove the pan from the heat. Add the lemon oil and peppermint oil and stir until well blended. Let cool to room temperature and bottle.

......................................................................

. . . . . . . . . . . . . . . . . . . . . . . . . . . . . . . . . . . . . . . . . . . . . . . . . . . . . . . . . . . .

❦ *Made with healing herbal extracts and moisture-balancing oil, Herbal Face Glow cleanses and revives the skin. This cleanser is gentle enough for everyday use.*

Makes 9 ounces

> 1 cup distilled water
> 1 tablespoon dried elder flowers
> 1 tablespoon dried lavender
> 1 tablespoon dried chamomile
> 1 tablespoon dried rosemary
> ½ tablespoon unscented glycerin soap
> 1 teaspoon jojoba oil
> 1 teaspoon witch hazel

Bring the water to a boil in a saucepan and add the dried elder flowers, lavender, chamomile, and rosemary. Remove the pan from the heat and let the herbs steep for one hour. Strain the herbs from the water and return to a gentle boil. Add the glycerin soap and stir until dissolved. Remove the saucepan from the heat and stir in the jojoba oil and witch hazel. Let cool to room temperature and bottle.

. . . . . . . . . . . . . . . . . . . . . . . . . . . . . . . . . . . . . . . . . . . . . . . . . . . . . . . . . . . .

# SCRUBBY SPONGE

..................................................................................................

❦ *Making your own colorful shower scrubbing sponges is fast and easy. These sponges work well with the shower gels and soaps described earlier. Scrubby sponges clean dirt and impurities from the skin and help exfoliate dry skin cells. They also make an excellent accessory when giving shower gels and soaps as gifts. They are made of a fabric called bridal illusion—the same material used to make bridal veils. It is fairly inexpensive, and you can purchase it at fabric stores. Bridal illusion comes in many colors that can be matched to coordinate with your shower gels and soaps. For example, if you make a lavender-scented shower gel, make a purple scrubby sponge to go along with it.*

> 1 yard bridal illusion
>    (available at fabric stores)
> 1 yard satin ribbon

Lay out the fabric on a flat surface. Fold it four times lengthwise. Start folding the fabric in half, bringing the two ends together. Fold in half again and again until you have a neat square of fabric about eight inches long. Take the ribbon and tie it tightly around the middle of the fabric square and secure it with a knot. Take the two ends of the ribbon and tie them in another knot one inch from the end. Fan out the folds of fabric until your sponge is full.

..................................................................................................

## BUBBLE BATH

...............................................................................

❦ *For a tub full of luxurious bubbles, try this great recipe for bubble bath. This formula can be scented by adding fifteen drops of any fragrance oil and colored with one drop of appropriate food coloring. Add a tablespoon of bubble bath to warm, running water.*

Makes 4½ ounces

⅓ cup purified water
2 tablespoons shampoo concentrate
(or substitute ¼ cup unscented shampoo
and increase salt to ½ teaspoon)
1 tablespoon liquid glycerin
¼ teaspoon table salt
15 drops fragrance oil
1 drop appropriate food coloring

Warm the water and pour into a ceramic bowl. Add the shampoo concentrate and stir until well blended. Add the glycerin, salt, fragrance oil, and food coloring, stirring until the mixture becomes a well-blended, thick liquid. Bottle.

❦ *Liquid glycerin can be purchased at drugstores in the first-aid section.*

...............................................................................

## VANILLA ROSE BUBBLE BATH GEL

..................................................................

❦ *This fragrant, bubbling bath gel is the perfect retreat after a long day. Pour one tablespoon into warm, running bath water and let the scented suds take you away.*

Makes 4½ ounces

> ¼ cup distilled water
> 2 tablespoons shampoo concentrate
> (or substitute ¼ cup unscented shampoo
> and increase salt to ½ teaspoon)
> 2 tablespoons rose water
> 1 tablespoon liquid glycerin
> ¼ teaspoon table salt
> 10 drops vanilla fragrance oil
> 4 drops rose fragrance oil

Warm the water and pour into a ceramic bowl. Add the shampoo concentrate and stir with a wire whisk until well blended. Add the rose water, liquid glycerin, salt, and fragrance oils and stir until well mixed. Bottle.

❦ *Liquid glycerin can be purchased at drugstores in the first-aid section.*

..................................................................

. . . . . . . . . . . . . . . . . . . . . . . . . . . . . . . . . . . . . . . . . . . . . . . . . . . . .

❦ *Treat your feet to a super-cleansing foot soak. Made with healing Australian tea tree oil, this formula soothes aches and itching, leaving your feet revitalized.*

Makes 8½ ounces

  1 cup distilled water
  2 teaspoons unscented glycerin soap
  1 teaspoon witch hazel
  ½ teaspoon tea tree oil

In a saucepan, boil the water and add the glycerin soap, stirring until dissolved. Remove the saucepan from the heat and add the witch hazel and tea tree oil, stirring until well blended. Let cool to room temperature and bottle. Pour a quarter cup of the mixture into a half gallon of warm water. Soak feet for twenty minutes.

## GLYCERIN HAND WASH

........................................................................

❦ *This recipe makes a liquid hand soap that is gentle enough for daily use.*

Makes 8 ½ ounces

> 1 cup distilled water
> 1 tablespoon unscented glycerin soap
> 15 drops fragrance oil (optional)

In a heavy saucepan, bring the water to a boil and add the glycerin soap, stirring until dissolved. Remove the saucepan from the heat and stir in the fragrance oil (if desired). Let the mixture cool to room temperature and store in a pump or squeeze bottle.

........................................................................

# CHAPTER FOUR

# *Hair Conditioners*

THE FOLLOWING recipes are for several types of cream rinses and conditioners for the hair. They have been specially developed to strengthen and protect. These formulas leave the hair looking healthy and shiny. For just pennies a bottle, you can make your own super batches, which have long shelf lives and make wonderful gifts.

Every hair conditioner on the market today (even the "organic" types) contains ingredients known as *humectants* and *finishing agents*, which make the hair feel soft and conditioned. These safe and nontoxic elements are derived from natural alcohols and ammonia through a special process. You can use any thick, unscented conditioner in these recipes. I suggest using cholesterol-type conditioners, which are very thick, have virtually no scent, and are available at most beauty supply shops. Fragrance oils can be purchased from health food stores or the suppliers listed in the marketplace section in the back of the book.

# FRUIT AND CREAM DAILY CONDITIONER

············································································

❦ *Fruit and Cream Daily Conditioner helps to remove dull build-up, restoring your hair's natural shine. Made with gentle apricot kernel oil and fruit oils, it protects and rehydrates the hair shaft. This conditioner can be used daily on all hair types.*

Makes 8 ounces

> ¾ cup distilled water
> ½ cup unscented cholesterol-type conditioner
> 2 teaspoons powdered milk
> 1 teaspoon apricot kernel oil
> 10 drops lemon oil
> 10 drops orange oil
> 10 drops strawberry fragrance oil

Warm the water and pour into a ceramic bowl. Add the cholesterol-type conditioner and stir with a wire whisk until well blended. Add the powdered milk, apricot kernel oil, lemon oil, orange oil, and strawberry fragrance oil and stir until well blended. Bottle.

············································································

## ALOE HAIR REJUVENATION TREATMENT

..........................................................

❦ *This super-hydrating formula moisturizes and helps protect your hair from the stresses of blow-drying and styling. This recipe was specially designed to restore moisture and body to the hair. Nourishing aloe vera helps to strengthen and restructure. Aloe Hair Rejuvenation Treatment is perfect for everyday use.*

Makes 8 ounces

> ¾ cup distilled water
> ½ cup unscented cholesterol-type conditioner
> 2 tablespoons aloe vera gel
> 1 teaspoon sweet almond oil
> 15 drops fragrance oil of choice (optional)

Warm the water and pour into a ceramic bowl. Add the cholesterol-type conditioner and stir until well blended. Add the aloe vera gel, sweet almond oil, and fragrance oil (if desired), stirring until well mixed. Bottle.

..........................................................

## PEPPERMINT HAIR PACK

........................................................................

❦ *This tingling hair treatment made with essential oils and stimulating peppermint deep-conditions your hair, leaving it silky soft. The formula was developed for occasional use, to repair and restore dry and damaged hair. Apply after shampooing to towel-dried hair and leave on for thirty minutes. Rinse thoroughly.*

Makes 6½ ounces

> ½ cup distilled water
> ½ cup unscented cholesterol-type conditioner
> 1 tablespoon jojoba oil
> 15 drops peppermint oil

Warm the water and pour into a ceramic bowl. Add the cholesterol-type conditioner and stir with a wire whisk until smooth. Add the jojoba oil and peppermint oil and stir until well blended. Bottle.

. . . . . . . . . . . . . . . . . . . . . . . . . . . . . . . . . . . . . . . . . . . . . . . . . . . . .

❦ *This lightweight cream rinse can be used every day for conditioning the hair. The formula contains rich, nourishing oils to lock in moisture and restore elasticity. With this recipe the exotic essence of a tropical rain forest is captured in a bottle and will leave your hair with the scent of pure paradise.*

Makes 8 ½ ounces

⅔ cup distilled water
⅔ cup unscented cholesterol-type conditioner
2 teaspoons jojoba oil
10 drops white ginger fragrance oil
4 drops coconut fragrance oil
2 drops jasmine fragrance oil
2 drops honeydew fragrance oil

Heat the water and pour into a ceramic bowl. Add the cholesterol-type conditioner and stir with a wire whisk until smooth. Add the jojoba oil and fragrance oils, stirring until well mixed. Bottle.

· · · · · · · · · · · · · · · · · · · · · · · · · · · · · · · · · · · · · · · · · · · · · · · · · · · · · · · · · · ·

❦ *This amazing leave-in conditioner helps restore moisture and shine to your hair. It also helps to protect the hair from styling damage. Spray this conditioner on damp hair after shampooing, or onto dry hair to help detangle or control frizzy fly-aways.*

Makes about 8 ounces

> 1 cup distilled water
> 2 teaspoons unscented cholesterol-type conditioner
> ½ teaspoon sweet almond oil
> 10 drops fragrance oil (optional)

Heat the water and pour into a ceramic bowl. Add the cholesterol-type conditioner and stir with a wire whisk until well blended. Add the sweet almond oil and fragrance oil (if desired) and stir until thoroughly mixed. Store in a spray-pump bottle.

# CHAPTER FIVE

# *Products for Children*

THE SPECIAL recipes in this chapter have been developed for children, to encourage them to take baths with great products that they love using. All of these formulas have been tested on real kids. The reactions I got when handing the little ones a bar of Bubble Gum Soap or a bottle of Tropical Orange Orangutan Conditioner were something like, "Cool!" or "Wow! Can I go try it now?"

Wrapping the products in colorful paper and decorating the bottles with stickers and such is almost as much fun as making the formulas. These products make wonderful presents and can be packaged as gift baskets and gift sets. My niece, who is eight years old, actually made her "own line" of kids' products based on my recipes and gave them to her friends and family as gifts. She always asks me when visiting, "Aunt Kelly? Can we make shampoo today? Pleeeease?" These wild and zany formulas are gentle and effective for cleansing young skin and can be made by children under adult supervision (a great rainy day activity!).

🐾 *Caution: Always store children's products in plastic bottles to avoid shattering glass.*

## GOOEY FUDGE SHAMPOO

..........................................................................................

*Who would have imagined washing their hair with chocolate fudge? This mild shampoo for kids is a gentle formula they love to use. Scented with real cocoa and vanilla fragrance oil, this easy-to-make recipe gets children excited about bath time.*

Makes 8 ounces

> ¾ cup distilled water
> ¼ cup shampoo concentrate
> > (or substitute with ½ cup unscented shampoo
> > and increase salt to 1 teaspoon)
> ½ teaspoon table salt
> 1 teaspoon powdered cocoa
> 20 drops vanilla fragrance oil

Warm the water and pour into a ceramic bowl. Add the shampoo concentrate and stir until dissolved. Add the salt, cocoa, and vanilla fragrance oil, stirring until thick and well blended. Bottle.

## GREEN SLIME SHOWER GEL

❦ *Kids love to clean up with this gentle body soap. It looks like slime, yet smells like fresh lemons. Taking a bath has never been more fun!*

Makes 7 ounces

¾ cup distilled water
2 tablespoons shampoo concentrate
  (or substitute with ¼ cup unscented shampoo
  and increase salt to 1½ teaspoons)
1 teaspoon table salt
15 drops lemon oil
1 drop green food coloring
1 drop yellow food coloring

Heat the water and add the shampoo concentrate. Stir until dissolved. Add the salt, lemon oil, and food colorings and stir until thick and well blended. Bottle.

. . . . . . . . . . . . . . . . . . . . . . . . . . . . . . . . . . . . . . . . . . . . . . . . . . . . . . . . .

❦ *This great-smelling grape soap is gentle to the skin. The finished soap has a marbleized look to it. You can mold the soap into an egg shape by filling two halves of a plastic Easter egg, or an old pantyhose container, with the freshly made soap. Close the two halves together and let it harden.*

Makes one Dinosaur Egg Bath Bar

>   4-ounce bar of Castile or baby soap
>   ¼ cup distilled water
>   2 teaspoons jojoba oil
>   15 drops grape flavor oil
>   1 drop violet food coloring

Shred the soap and set aside. In a heavy saucepan, bring the water to a boil and add the shredded soap, stirring until it forms a sticky mass. Remove the saucepan from the heat and add the jojoba oil, grape flavor oil, and food coloring, stirring until well blended. Spoon into an egg-shaped soap mold and let set for four hours or until hardened.

. . . . . . . . . . . . . . . . . . . . . . . . . . . . . . . . . . . . . . . . . . . . . . . . . . . . . . . . .

........................................................................................

❦ *Screeching Monkey Soap, made especially for kids, will have them screeching for more! Made with gentle glycerin soap, skin-softening coconut oil, and a wild banana fragrance, your little monkeys will go ape at bath time!*

Makes one bar

> 4-ounce bar of unscented glycerin soap
> 1 teaspoon coconut oil
> 10 drops banana flavor oil
> 1 drop yellow food coloring

Melt the soap in a heavy saucepan over low heat until liquefied. Remove the saucepan from the heat and stir in the coconut oil, banana flavor oil, and coloring until well blended. Pour into a mold and let set for three hours or until hardened.

❦ *Flavor oils can be ordered from suppliers listed in the marketplace section at the back of the book.*

........................................................................................

## BUBBLE GUM SOAP

........................................................................

❧ *Kids love to suds up with this fun soap. Made with gentle glycerin soap and a scent they'll love, this bubbling Bubble Gum Soap is a bath-time treat!*

Makes one bar

> 4-ounce bar of unscented glycerin soap
> 1 teaspoon sweet almond oil
> 15 drops bubble gum flavor oil
> > (or substitute 10 drops vanilla and
> > 5 drops cherry fragrance oils)
> 1 drop red food coloring (optional)

In a heavy saucepan over low heat, melt the soap until liquefied. Remove the saucepan from the heat and add the sweet almond oil, bubble gum flavor oil, and food coloring (if desired), stirring until well blended. Pour into a mold and let set for three hours or until hardened.

❧ *Flavor oils can be ordered from suppliers listed in the marketplace section at the back of the book.*

........................................................................

# SILLY STRAWBERRY SHAMPOO

........................................................................

*❦ Kids of all ages love the fragrance of Silly Strawberry Shampoo. The essence of fresh strawberries is captured in this delightful shampoo.*

Makes 8 ounces

> ¾ cup distilled water
> ¼ cup shampoo concentrate
> (or substitute ½ cup unscented shampoo
> and increase salt to 1 teaspoon)
> ½ teaspoon table salt
> 15 drops strawberry fragrance oil
> 1 drop red food coloring (optional)

Add the shampoo concentrate to warm water. Stir until well blended. Add the salt, strawberry fragrance oil, and food coloring (if desired) and stir until smooth. Bottle.

........................................................................

# BLUE RASPBERRY SHOWER GEL

❦ *This wild-looking shower gel smells of sweet raspberries. The added aloe vera gel is gentle on young and sensitive skin.*

Makes 8 ounces

> ¾ cup distilled water
> 2 tablespoons shampoo concentrate
> (or substitute ¼ cup unscented shampoo
> and increase salt to 1½ teaspoons)
> 2 tablespoons aloe vera gel
> 1 teaspoon table salt
> 15 drops raspberry fragrance oil
> 1 drop blue food coloring (optional)

Add the shampoo concentrate to warm water, stirring until well mixed. Add the aloe vera gel, salt, raspberry fragrance oil, and food coloring (if desired). Stir until thick and well blended. Bottle.

························································································

❦ *This gentle cream rinse is specially formulated for children. Fabulously fragranced with orange oil, it keeps young hair healthy and detangled.*

Makes 8 ounces

> ¾ cup distilled water
> ½ cup unscented cholesterol-type conditioner
> 15 drops orange oil
> 1 drop orange food coloring (optional)

Add the conditioner concentrate to warm water. Stir until well mixed. Add the orange oil and food coloring (if desired). Stir until well blended. Bottle.

························································································

# TROPICAL ORANGE ORANGUTAN CONDITIONER

# CHAPTER SIX

# *Gift Wrapping*

## Presenting and Displaying Your Gifts

CREATIVE PACKAGING of your homemade toiletries makes your gift even more special. By wrapping your creations decoratively, you can make your already spectacular gifts look even more appealing and fabulous. The ideas in this section will help you to present your gifts safely and beautifully.

### *Bottles*

Bottles are perfect for storing lotions, creams, perfumes, and other liquid luxuries. You can find bottles in many different shapes and sizes, from plain plastic to fancy perfume atomizers. I've found beautiful glass bottles in shades of blue and even fuchsia. I fill the bottles with my liquid creations and tie a beautiful ribbon around the bottle neck. Gold French ribbon and brightly colored satin ribbons look really spectacular. To create a natural look you can tie a piece of raffia around the top. For an elegant touch, hang a fancy tassle on your bottle. Antique-style perfume atomizers make wonderful containers for perfumes. You can order bottles and atomizers by mail or buy them from import shops. Silk flowers add a nice touch to your bottled creations. You can slip their stems under your piece of ribbon, which will hold them securely in place.

Old bottles can be recycled and reused. To remove paper labels, fill a large bowl with warm water and about an ounce of dish-washing liquid. Drop in the bottle and let it soak for a few hours. The old labels should lift off. Scrub off any glue residue with a vegetable brush. To remove silk-screened printing from a bottle, dab on an acetone nail polish remover with some cotton balls. Last year I made an assortment of homemade perfumes and lotions as a gift for a friend. I filled miniature perfume bottles with my own custom blends and filled several travel-size shampoo bottles with lotions and creams. Each bottle was labeled and had a thin piece of colorful satin ribbon tied around the top. For another friend I made a "country" theme assortment of lotions and bath oils and put them in small jelly jars. Each jar top was covered with a circle of gingham fabric and tied with a matching ribbon. I wrote my labels by hand to give each jar a casual, cozy look.

## Labeling

You should always label your products, whether giving them as gifts or keeping them for yourself. Write the name of the product (for example, "Herbal Face Glow") on the label and secure it to the container. You can use plain white labels or purchase decorative labels. To waterproof your labels, rub a white candle firmly over the writing. This leaves a wax coating that will help prevent ink smears if it gets wet.

You can also make beautiful decoupage labels using plain, white computer labels. Cut out pictures from magazines of flowers and other images that you like. You can also use stickers such as metallic stars or zany designs. Using spray glue, spray the back side of the cut-outs and press them around the edges of the label, leaving enough space in the center of the label on which to write.

Paints and paint pens can be used to write directly on the bottles. Make sure that the paint you choose will stick to the type of bottle you've chosen. Another good idea is to list on the label the ingredients used in the product. This will help friends avoid using a product to which they're allergic. Finally, write any special usage instructions on your label; for example, if a specific amount is suggested, you might write "add one tablespoon to warm bath water."

*Fancy boxes*

Packaging your creations in fancy boxes doesn't have to cost a fortune. You can turn an ordinary shoe box into a treasured gift by covering it with self-sticking fabric or by using simple decoupage techniques. I sometimes cover shoe boxes with decorative contact paper and have even used wall paper with interesting patterns. Boxes can also be spray painted. Metallic gold and silver are perfect colors to use around the holidays. For more ideas, get a book about box decorating, which you can find at craft and fabric stores.

## Wrapping Your Soaps

Soap needs to be protected. I always wrap my soaps with clear cellophane, twenty-four hours after removing the soaps from their molds. The cellophane can be secured with a piece of clear tape if necessary. For more decorative wrapping, seal your soap in cellophane, then wrap it up in an eight-inch by eight-inch piece of lace and tie it closed with a satin ribbon. I have also wrapped soaps in tissue and wrapping paper and secured the paper with a decorative label or sticker. The possibilities are limitless, so have fun with your imagination.

## Sealing and Packing

Proper sealing and packing are vital if you plan to mail your creations. If you are mailing bottles, always make sure that the caps and lids are securely closed. To seal a cork-type bottle, the cork should fit tightly, then for extra security use a glue gun around the edges (the glue will peel off when the cork is removed). When packing gift baskets or boxes, choose a basket or box that your creations fit into with very little room left over. Cushion any spaces with wadded-up tissue paper, bubble wrap, or raffia packing material. Then seal the box. The contents should not move around inside if you've packed them well. Give the box a test shake before mailing. Always mark your boxes "fragile" or "this end up" to help ensure that they arrive safely.

## Other Ideas

Luxury gift sets make impressive gifts and are inexpensive. Fill a box with an assortment of bath products and add a tea cup with some tea bags.

Theme baskets are another type of gift to make. Fill a basket with lotions and bath products all of the same scent, such as rose or lemon. Tuck a few silk flowers in with your package. To hold your bottles in place, use raffia packing material. It comes in many bright colors and will look great! Once you've packed your basket, use a large piece of cellophane to wrap the entire basket and secure it with a large, colorful ribbon. Cellophane gift wrap can be found with regular wrapping paper in the stores and comes in many bright colors as well as clear.

A good way to wrap dry or powdered luxuries such as bath powder and bath salts is to make your own envelopes. Take a regular envelope and unfold it to use as a pattern. Lay it on a piece of decorative wrapping paper and trace the edges. Cut the wrapping paper and fold it into an envelope, using tape to secure the edges and seams. Fill it with powder or bath salts and seal. Stick a pretty label on the outside of the envelope.

# Marketplace

SOME OF the ingredients and supplies for making cosmetics at home can be hard to find if you don't live in a big city. The following are listings of manufacturers and suppliers who sell cosmetic supplies by mail.

Aroma Vera
5901 Rodeo Rd.
Los Angeles, California 90016-4312
*Essential oils, aromatherapy supplies, floral waters*

General Bottle Supply
1930 E. 51st St.
Los Angeles, California 90058
Phone: (800) 782-0198
*Free catalog; wide selection of glass, plastic, and perfume bottles*

General Wax and Candle Company
P.O. Box 9398
North Hollywood, California 91609
Phone: (800) 543-0642
*Beeswax, molds, candle-making supplies*

Lorann Oils
P.O. Box 22009
4518 Aurelius Rd.
Lansing, Michigan 48909-2009
Phone: (800) 248-1302
*Perfume oils, flavor oils, soap-, candy-, and candle-making supplies*

Mountain Rose Herbs
20818 High St.
North San Juan, California 95960
*Herbs, oils, bottles, clays, labels, books, aloe vera,
lanolin, glycerin, beeswax, floral waters*

Pourette
P.O. Box 15220
6910 Roosevelt Way N.E.
Seattle, Washington 98115
*Soap- and candle-making supplies, unscented soap*

San Francisco Herb Company
250 14th St.
San Francisco, California 94103
Phone: (800) 227-4530
*Dried herbs and flowers, potpourri ingredients*

Sunburst Bottle Company
5710 Auburn Blvd., Ste. #7
Sacramento, California 95841
Phone: (916) 348-5576
*Send $2 for catalog; wide selection of glass, plastic, and perfume bottles*

Tri-Ess Sciences
1020 W. Chestnut St.
Burbank, California 91506
Phone: (818) 848-7838
*Scientific equipment and small amounts of chemical supplies*

Valley Hills Press
3400 Earles Fork Rd.
Sturgis, Mississippi 39769
Phone: (800) 323-7102
*Books about soap-making*

Victorian Essence
P.O. Box 1220
Arcadia, California 91077
Phone: (888) 446-5455
Web site: www.Victorian-Essence.com
*Shampoo concentrate and shampoo-making kits*

## A

Almond and Vanilla Soap, 19
Aloe Hair Rejuvenation Treatment, 59
Aloe and Green Apple Shower Gel, 44

## B

Banana, Screeching Monkey Soap, 67
Berry and Peach Gardener's Hand Cream
    14–15
Blue Raspberry Shower Gel, 70
Bottles, 73–74
Bubble Bath, 53–54
Bubble Gum Soap, 68

## C

Castile soap, 2
Chamomile and Peppermint Soap, 10–11
Cinnamon Soap, 24
City Shampoo, 38–39

Coconut and Vanilla Hair Repair
    Shampoo, 36
Coffee and Cream Soap, 24
Conditioners and cream rinses, 57–62, 71
Creamsicle Soap, 20–21

## D

Detangling Conditioner, 62
Dinosaur Egg Bath Bar, Purple, 66

## E

Easy Shower Gel, 48
Emergency Shampoo, 40
English Lavender and Cream Shower Gel, 46

## F

Face wash, 49–51
Fancy boxes, 76

Foot bath, 55
Fruit and Cream Daily Conditioner, 58
Fudge Shampoo, Gooey, 64

### G

Gardener's Friend Hand Soap, 13
Gardener's Hand Cream, 14–15
Gel Shampoo Base, 34
Georgia Peach Shower Gel, 45
Gift wrapping, 73–78
Glycerin Hand Wash, 56
Glycerin soap, 2
Gooey Fudge Shampoo, 64
Green Apple and Aloe Shower Gel, 44
Green Slime Shower Gel, 65

### H

Hair Conditioners, 57–62, 71
Hand Wash, 57
Herbal Face Glow, 51

Herbal Fantasy Soap, 8–9
Honey and Rose Water Face Wash, 49

### I

Ingredients (where to locate), 4, 31–32, 57,
    79–82

### J

Jasmine and Rice Bran Body Bar, 17

### K

Kid's products, 63–71

### L

Labeling, 75
Lavender Shower Gel, 46
Leave-In Conditioner, 62
Lemon Rinse, Old-Fashioned, 42

Lemon Loofah Soap, 22–23
Lemon and Mint Face Wash, 50
Lemon Sparkle Shampoo, 35
Liquid Shampoo and Shower Gel Base, 33

## M

Miracle Hair Detangler, 62
Molding soaps, 3
Mud Soap, 16

## O

Oatmeal Soap, 6–7
Old-Fashioned Lemon Rinse, 42
Old-Fashioned Shampoo, 41
Orange Orangutan Conditioner, Tropical, 71

## P

Peach and Berry Gardener's Hand Cream,
    14–15
Peach Shower Gel, 45
Peaches and Cream Bath Bar, 18

Peppermint and Chamomile Soap, 10–11
Peppermint Clarifying Shampoo, 37
Peppermint Hair Pack, 60
Purple Dinosaur Egg Bath Bar, 66

## R

Raspberry Oat Powder Soap, 26
Rice Bran and Jasmine Body Bar, 17
Rose Cold Cream Soap, 28
Rose Water and Honey Face Wash, 49

## S

Screeching Monkey Soap, 67
Scrubby Sponge, 52
Sealing and Packing, 77
Shampoos, 31–42, 64, 69
Soap on a rope, 4–5
Soaps, 1–13
Strawberry Shampoo, Silly, 69
Suppliers, 79–82

## T

Tea Tree Oil Foot Bath, 55
Tomato and Baking Soda Soap, 27
Tropical Rain Forest Cream Rinse, 61

## V

Vanilla and Almond Soap, 19
Vanilla and Coconut Hair Repair Shampoo, 36
Vanilla Rose Bubble Bath Gel, 54